MW01205406

Computer Programming For Beginners

Learn The Basics of Java, SQL, C, C++, C#, Python, HTML, CSS and Javascript

Introduction

The art of writing computer programs effectively and efficiently is referred to as computer programming. Typically, a computer program is a sequence of instructions given to the computer for performing a specific task. However, how these computer programs have to be written, compiled and executed is programming language dependent.

If you see assembly code or programs that are written for and executed on 8085/8086 processors, you will realize that it is a list of instruction codes with the allowable data and parameters, written in the sequence in which they have to be performed. A sample 8085 assembly program to perform addition of two numbers is given below.

8085 Assembly Program for Adding Two 8-bit Numbers
—

MVI B, 00   /*Moves the value 00 to Register B*/

LDA 4151   /*Loads the number stored at 4151 to the
Accumulator*/

MOV C, A   /*Moves the contents of Accumulator to
Register C*/

LDA 4152   /* Loads the number stored at 4152 to the
Accumulator*/

ADD C   /*Add the contents of Accumulator
and Register C*/

JNC LOOP   /*If there is no carry, jump to instruction
with label LOOP*/

INR B   /*Increment the value of Register B*/

LOOP: STA 4153   /* *Loads the contents of the Accumulator to location 4153*/*

MOV A, B   /**Moves the contents of Register B to Accumulator*/*

STA 4154   /* *Loads the contents of the Accumulator to location 4154*/*

HLT   /**Halt the execution of the program*/*

The opcodes corresponding to these instructions are looked up in the manual, which are then punched in. Internally, these opcodes are converted into their binary forms and form the language that the processor in the computer understands. Evidently, addition of two 8-bit numbers is the simplest task that you can perform. Considering the lines of code and effort required for performing this operation, you can well imagine the amount of effort that will go into writing complicated programs in this manner.

With the advent of I/O devices and advancement in the operating system capabilities of computers, the concept of programming languages and development environments came into existence. A programming language makes programming simpler in the sense that the programmer is only expected to design the logic and write the program in accordance with the syntax and using language-specific keywords.

Thus, computer programs are written in plain English without the need for you to lookup the opcodes manual and punch in all the codes to execute a program. Learning to write computer programs can be fun if you take up the right approach and this shall be the objective of this book. We attempt to provide you a simple, easy to follow and practically sound approach to computer programming.

Most novice learners face serious issues in learning computer programming. This book has been specifically designed to cater the needs of a new learner as well as a skilled programmer. However, a word of advice for new learners is that you must go through the book a couple of times to get a better understanding of the subject. This shall help you transition from a novice to expert. The first reading will help you form a foundation, which can be solidified by a second reading. — *Read book two times!!*

With that said, it is crucial to mention that this book requires no previous knowledge of computer programming. If you have had some exposure to using computers and possess a basic know-how of the peripherals and I/O devices attached to the computer like keyboard, mouse and monitor, you are ready to get started.

♥ **Copyright 2017 - All rights reserved.**

This document is geared towards providing exact and reliable information in regards to the topic and issue covered. The publication is sold with the idea that the publisher is not required to render accounting, officially permitted, or otherwise, qualified services. If advice is necessary, legal or professional, a practiced individual in the profession should be ordered.

- From a Declaration of Principles which was accepted and approved equally by a Committee of the American Bar Association and a Committee of Publishers and Associations.

In no way is it legal to reproduce, duplicate, or transmit any part of this document in either electronic means or in printed format. Recording of this publication is strictly prohibited and any storage of this document is not allowed unless with written permission from the publisher. All rights reserved.

The information provided herein is stated to be truthful and consistent, in that any liability, in terms of inattention or otherwise, by any usage or abuse of any policies, processes, or directions contained within is the solitary and utter responsibility of the recipient reader. Under no circumstances will any legal responsibility or blame be held against the publisher for any reparation, damages, or monetary loss due to the information herein, either directly or indirectly.

Respective authors own all copyrights not held by the publisher.

The information herein is offered for informational purposes solely, and is universal as so. The presentation of the information is without contract or any type of guarantee assurance.

The trademarks that are used are without any consent, and the publication of the trademark is without permission or backing by the trademark owner. All trademarks and brands within this book are for clarifying purposes only and are the owned by the owners themselves, not affiliated with this document.

Table of Contents

Chapter 1: Basics of Programming

Before we take a plunge into the world of computer programming, let us take a closer look at what computer programs are and what they are supposed to be. The standard defining of a computer program is as follows:

A sequence of instructions for performing a particular task that has been written in a specific programming language is commonly referred to as a computer program.

As you can see in the given definition, two phrases have been written in bold namely, 'sequence of instructions' and 'programming language'. To understand the meaning and significance of these two terms, let us take an example. For instance, you have a household help and you have to tell her the procedure to prepare 2 cups of coffee. What will be the set of instructions that you will give to her? In all probability, you will tell her something like this –

1. Firstly, take two cups and keep them on the kitchen slab.

2. Take a boiling pan and using one of these cups for measurement, add two cups of water to it.

3. Switch on the stove.

4. Put the boiling pan on medium heat and wait until the water starts boiling.

5. In the two cups, add 1 teaspoon of coffee, 1 teaspoon of sugar and 1 teaspoon of milk powder.

6. Add boiling water to the cups.

7. Lastly, serve.

The seven steps mentioned above form what can be called 'human program'. It is a set of instructions that you have given to a human to perform a specific task. Since the language used for this human program is English, the programming language used for writing this human program is English. If your household help doesn't understand English, this human program will fail. Therefore, you will have to translate this program to the language she understands, which can be French, Arabic, Hindi, Spanish or any other language for that matter.

Analogously, when you have to tell the computer to do something for you, you have to give it a set of instructions in the language that it can understand. The language that it understands is the computer programming language and the set of instructions written in that language and given to the computer to perform a specific task is simply a computer program.

There are some other terms that you may also encounter in the world of computer programming. One such term is software. A computer program is usually also referred to as software. Besides this, you may also see phrases like source code and program coding. These are terms usually used for referring to the set of instructions written in a computer program.

Computer Programs

Computer programs are the heart and soul of a computer. The hardware is just a dead body unless you have active computer programs running on the system. All the capabilities of the computer can be used only after you tell the computer what it should do for you in the form of computer programs.

We unconsciously use many computer programs everyday. For instance, Google Chrome or Internet Explorer that you use to browse Internet is a computer program. The chat programs you use on your computer or mobile phone is a computer program. Moreover, the voice calls and SMS capabilities of mobile phones are also computer programs. You name it and there is a computer program associated with it. Whenever and wherever you use a computer to do a task, you are using a computer program.

Since computer programming is a skilled job, the individual who has an expertise in computer programming is referred to as a computer programmer. Depending on the programming language in which the computer programmer has expertise, he or she is called Python/C/HTML/Java/CSS/SQL/JavaScript programmer.

Algorithm

Now that you are thorough with the concept of computer program, you can simply relate computer programming to the process and art of writing computer programs. These programs should not only perform the specified task, but they should also do them well. This is where the concept of effective and efficient programming came into existence.

In order to make the process of program designing simpler, several approaches have been designed. The systematic procedure developed to solve a problem is called an algorithm. It is one of the most effective approaches for creation of a sequence of well-defined instructions aimed towards performing a task. You will hear this term just as much as you shall counter computer programs as they essentially go hand in hand.

In simple words, an algorithm is an English language equivalent of the computer program, written in the form of a list, by the programmer, before transforming it into a programming language – specific code. A sample algorithm has been given below to help you understand how an algorithm typically looks like. This algorithm given below computes the largest number from a list of numbers.

Algorithm for Computing Largest Number From Given List of Numbers

1. Get the given list of numbers.

2. Assume a variable L, which will hold the largest number.

3. Initialize L with the first number of the list.

4. Go to the next number of the list.

5. If L is less than this number, put this new number in L

6. Repeat step 4 and step 5 till the list is completely scanned.

7. Print L on the screen

This is a raw algorithm written in simple language to make it easy to understand for beginners. There is a standard procedure that needs to be followed for writing algorithms. However, this is part of advanced programming fundamentals and is beyond the scope of this book.

Programming Languages

Just like we have innumerable languages that are used for communication between humans, scientists have developed a plethora of computer programming languages to serve and meet the varied requirements of developers and applications. We will introduce some of the key languages to you in the chapters to come. A list of the programming languages that we shall cover is as follows –

1. Java

2. SQL

3. C

4. C++

5. C#

6. Python

7. HTML

8. CSS

9. JavaScript

In order to understand the concept of programming languages, their structure and how they work, let us look at English, which is a standard human interface language. It is used by billions of people around the world to communicate with each other. As we know, English language makes words from a set of alphabets and these words are used to make sentences.

In order to make sure that the sentences are understandable to one and all, several grammar rules have to be applied. Besides this, language elements like conjunctions, verbs, nouns and adverbs, in addition to several others, have to be kept in mind while forming sentences. Likewise, other languages like French, Spanish, Russian, Arabic or Hindi also have their own set of rules that need to be followed for effective communication between two humans.

In the same manner, computer languages also have rules and elements that need to be understood before you can write programs to communicate with the computer. Some of these basic elements are as follows –

- Syntax
- Data types
- Keywords
- Variables
- Operators
- Loops
- Decision Making
- Program organization elements like Functions
- File I/O
- Programming environment

Most of the languages that we shall deal with in this book will have most of these elements. However, how they are included in the programming language varies. In this book, we shall introduce you to the different programming languages listed above and deal with the different elements and advanced programming concepts specific to the programming language in books specifically written for the language.

Chapter 2: Programming Environment

Although, programming environment does not form one of the core elements of a programming language, it would not be wrong to state that it is one of the prerequisites that you need to learn and get acquainted with even before you have written your first program. You will never know if your program is right or wrong unless you have a programming environment that can test the same for you. This is the reason why we are going to introduce you to programming environment before we jump to languages.

Simply, programming environment is software that will allow you to create, compile and execute computer programs on the system. It is an interface between the programmer and the computer, which will convert the programs that you will write into the computer's language and ask it to execute the same for you. Therefore, before you pick up any programming language, be sure to enquire about the required programming environment and how the same can be set up on the computer that you intend to use for your programming course.

Digging deeper into the programming environment and its setup, it is made up of three basic elements namely text editor, compiler and interpreter. In all probability, you will need all these three components for your course. So, before you go searching for them, let us help you understand what they exactly are and why you will need them.

Text Editor

A text editor is a simple text program that will allow you to create text files in which you will write you code. Depending on the programming language you are working on, the extension of the text file will change. For instance, if you programming in C language, your text files will have the extension .c.

If you are working on a Windows machine, you can simply search for Notepad in the search bar and use it as a text editor for your programs. You can also explore Notepad++ for some advanced options. It is freely available and you will just need to download and install it on your machine. On the other hand, if you are a Mac user, you can explore text editor options like BBEdit and TextEdit.

Compiler

Now that you have written the program and you are all ready to test if you have written it correctly or not, you have to give it to the computer and see if it understands what you are trying to communicate. However, the computer only understands binary language and what you have written is far from what it can directly digest. Therefore, this file needs to be converted into binary format.

If you have made syntactical errors and not followed the rules of the programming language, the compiler will not be able to make this conversion smoothly and will raise an error message for you. Therefore, the compiler is a program that checks if you have followed the syntactical rules of the chosen programming language and converts the text file into its binary form. Moreover, this process of conversion is referred to as compilation.

Most programming languages like C, Java, C++ and Pascal, besides many others require compilation and you will need to install their respective compilers before you can execute any programs written using them.

Interpreter

Unlike the programming languages mentioned above, there are some other programming languages like Python and Perl that do not require compiler. Therefore, instead of a compiler, they need an interpreter, which is also software. The interpreter simply reads the program from the text file and as it parses the file, it converts the contents of the file and executes them. If you are working on any such programming languages, remember to install the corresponding interpreter on your system before starting.

If you haven't worked with a computer before or have little to no experience in installing software on the computer, technical advice from an expert is recommended. However, be sure to do the installation yourself, as it will help you build an acquaintance with the device that you will work with in the near future.

Besides this, if your computer does not support installation of any of the programming environment elements, you can also make use of the online compilers and interpreters that are available for all the different programming languages nowadays. All you need is a good Internet connection and a web browser to open these online facilities and get started with your programming lessons and practice sessions right away.

Chapter 3: Java

One of the most popular programming languages today is Java. Originally, Java was developed by Sun Microsystems under the leadership of James Gosling. The first milestone in this programming language development was the release of Java 1.0 [J2SE], the core component of the Java platform, in the year 1995.

Java has come a long way since then and presently most of us are working on Java SE 8. In accordance with the varied applicability and wide realm of use of this programming language, many Java platforms have been developed. Some of these include J2ME (J2 Mobile Edition) for development of mobile applications and J2EE (J2 Enterprise Edition) for applications related to Enterprises.

The biggest USP of this programming language and fundamentally, the intent behind its development, is the fact that it is machine independent. You have to write the program once and you can run the executable anywhere you like. In addition to this, Java also has some extremely unique and useful features, which are as follows –

Java is platform-independent
Programming languages like C and C++ are complied into binary forms that are machine-specific. On the other hand, when a Java file is compiled, a byte-code file is generated, which is platform-independent and can be run on any device. This file can be circulated over the web and all you need to run it, is a Java Virtual Machine (JVM).

Java is object-oriented
This programming language is based on the object model. Hence, everything in Java is an object. This allows infinite extensibility.

Independent of the architecture

The byte-code of the Java file can be run on any processor or hardware configuration for that matter. All you need to run the Java file is the Java runtime environment. This makes Java, architecture-independent.

Portable

The fact that Java's object code can be run on any architecture or platform makes it a portable programming language. The Java compiler is written in C and the portability boundary is clean, implemented with the help of the POSIX subset.

Simple and Secure

The language has been designed in such a manner that new and experienced programmers can pick it up quickly and start programming in the least time possible. If you have a little idea about Object Oriented Programming (OOP), learning Java shall not be an uphill task. Besides this, Java is essentially secure in the sense it uses public-key encryption for authentication and thus, it allows development of virus-proof systems.

Multithreaded Environment

With the help of the multithreaded functionality, it is possible to write programs that can perform many tasks at the same time. One of the most important applications of such an environment is the implementation of interactive request management.

Robust

Error checking is performed during compilation as well as run-time. As a result, error-prone scenarios are primarily avoided.

High performance

Java Runtime Environment makes use of Just-In-Time Compilers. This gives it the high performance that Java boasts of.

Code is interpreted, not compiled

Java programs are directly translated and executed. This makes the process lightweight and incremental in the sense that the code is not stored anywhere, in this case. Moreover, this also makes the development process quick.

Dynamic
Java processes carry a lot of runtime information to allow features that require runtime resolution of accesses to objects. As a result, Java is much more dynamic when compared to C and C++.

Distributed
With the advent of Internet, programming languages need to cater the demand for distributed storage and processing. Java has been developed keeping this requirement in mind.

How did it all happen?

James Gosling initiated the project that finally led to the development of Java in the year 1991. A lot of random words like Green and Oak were scanned before giving this programming language the name 'Java'. The first release of Java came four years later in the year 1995 with the tagline 'Write Once, Run Anywhere'.

In fact, Sun also provided run-times at no cost on most of the popular platforms. With the rising popularity and demand for open source solutions, Sun decided to make most of the Java and related software free under the GNU license. By the year 2007, all of the components of Java were declared open source.

Prerequisites for Learning Java

First things first, you will need a computer with a standard configuration to support the following software solutions –

- Java JDK 8
- Text Editor
- Operating System like Windows/Linux/Mac

Like we mentioned previously, you may override the whole installation process and run the java code on one of the online platforms.

Getting Started with Java

To help you give a basic idea about how Java programming is done, we have given the simple Java code below. This code prints 'Hello World!' upon execution.

```java
public class SampleProgram {

  public static void main(String []args) {

    System.out.println("Hello World!");

  }

}
```

Since, Java implements OOPs concepts, you need to create a class for your program. In the example shown above, we have created a class SampleProgram. Program execution begins from the main method of the class. Therefore, the print statement for displaying 'Hello World!' on the screen is written inside the main method. You can write this code in a text file named SampleProgram.java. This file can be compiled and executed to get the desired output.

What next?

Now that you have all the background knowledge and setup ready to get started with the Java tutorial, we recommend you to pick up our book on 'Java Programming' and become an expert Java programmer.

Chapter 4: SQL

SQL or Structured Query Language is a programming languages used for database. It is primarily used for management and retrieval of data from relational databases. This chapter shall give you a basic understanding of SQL and how it works. In order to gain a better understanding of SQL, you must read about databases, particularly RDBMS.

Understanding SQL

In simple terms SQL is a programming language that is used for performing operations on databases. These operations include database creation/deletion, row creation/deletion/modification and data retrieval. Although there are many version of SQL that you might have heard about, SQL is an ANSI standard programming language.

Codd gave the relational model for databases in the year 1970. Four years later, structured query language for RDBMSs appeared. As far as Relational Database Management Systems (RDBMS) are concerned, SQL is the standard language. Supported RDBMSs include SQL Server, MS Access, MySQL, Sybase, Oracle, Postgres and Informix. There are many versions of SQL used. One example of this is MS Access version of SQL.

Key reasons for choosing SQL as the standard language for RDBMS management are as follows –

- Data can be described.

- Data can be accessed.

- Data can be defined and manipulated.

- It can be integrated with other languages with the help of compiler, libraries and SQL modules.

- Databases and tables can be created and deleted.

- Functions, stored procedures and views can be created.

- The user can set permissions on views, procedures and tables.

SQL Process and Commands

Typically, whenever you instruct the system to execute a SQL query for the concerned relational database management system, it is the job of the SQL engine to see how it needs to interpret the task. Moreover, the system finds out the most efficient way for carrying out the task. Several components of the system are involved in carrying out this task, which include –

- Optimization Engines

- Query Dispatcher

- SQL Query Engine

- Classic Query Engine

Besides these, there are some other components as well that are involved in the execution process. However, we have decided to keep them out for simplicity sake. The classic query engine tackles all queries that are non-SQL in nature. It has been kept in place because the SQL engine cannot handle logical files.

In order to create SQL queries, you need to first get acquainted with SQL commands. The basic commands that you need to know at this stage are CREATE, INSERT, DELETE, UPDATE, DROP and SELECT. The table shown below described the function of each of these commands.

Command	Function
CREATE	This command is used to create an object, view or table in the database.
INSERT	This command creates a new record in the database.
DELETE	This command is used for deleting records from the database.
ALTER	This command is used for making modifications to an existing table in the database.
DROP	This command is used for deleting objects, views or tables, usually created using CREATE.
SELECT	This command is used for retrieving data from a table existing in the database.
UPDATE	This command is used for updating records in the database.
REVOKE	This command is used for taking away already given privileges to a user.
GRANT	This command is used for granting a privilege to a user.

The commands UPDATE and DELETE are classified as part of Data Manipulation Language (DML). On the other hand, commands GRANT and REVOKE are classified as part of Data Control Language (DCL). All the other commands mentioned in the table shown above are classified as part of Data Definition Language (DDL).

Prerequisites for Learning SQL

Ideally, to compile and execute SQL programs or run queries with Oracle 11g RDBMS, you need a setup on the local system. However, with the advent of online solutions like Coding Ground and many others, you can run SQL programs online. You can try these options out if you are not willing to spend the time and energy required to prepare your setup.

Running your First SQL Query

On the console, you need to first create a database using the following query:

CREATE DATABASE sampledb;

Now that you have created a database, you have to tell the system that you want to work in this database. For this, you need to fire the query:

USE sampledb;

You can now create a table inside this database using the query:

CREATE TABLE Person (

> *IDPerson int,*

> *LName varchar(255),*

> *FName varchar(255),*

> *City varchar(255)*

);

The next step is to insert records into this table, Person. You can do so using the query:

INSERT INTO Person

> *(IDPerson, LName, FName, City)*

VALUES

(1,"Sparrow", "Jack", "Bali"),

(2,"Daniel", "Edward", "Manila"),

A standard query for displaying all the records of the table, Person is given below.

*SELECT * FROM Person*

If you have reached so far and can see queries executing for you, then you have achieved a basic understanding of how SQL queries are run.

What next?

Moving forward, you can try new commands and more complicated queries. However, for that, you will need to brush through the commands and operations. We recommend you to go through our book on 'SQL' for basic and advanced lessons on the language.

Chapter 5: C

C is a computer programming language that is described using three keywords namely 'imperative', 'procedural' and 'general-purpose'. This programming language came into existence while Dennis Richie was developing the Unix Operating System in the year 1972.

Since then, C has grown to become the most widely used programming language in the software and programming industry. With the growing popularity of Java among modern programmers, C has had to share the stage with this programming language in the last few decades.

C programming language is usually the first programming language taught to students pursuing computer science. The reason for this is that the fundamentals of C are used in almost every other programming language that you will ever encounter in your programming career.

This makes C an important programming language to learn. Although, learning C does not require any prior knowledge, some knowledge about programming language fundamentals and basic data structure concepts can fast track your learning curve. Apart from the desktop compiler that is available for C program compilation and execution, you can also try one of the online compilation portals available nowadays.

Getting To Know C

Like we mentioned previously, C was developed as a byproduct of the implementation of Unix Operating System. Originally, DEC PDP-11 computer was used for its implementation. So, why was 'C' called 'C'? This programming language is considered to have evolved from another programming language 'B', which was released in 1970.

Kernighan and Richie updated this original version in the year 1978, which is also referred to as the K&R Standard C. Besides the Unix operating system, Unix applications and the C compiler have been written in C programming language. The American National Standard Institute (ANSI) standardized the language in the 1988 and since then, this language has been in use for system programming. In fact, MySQL and Linux operating system have also been written in C.

The popularity of C can be attributed to the following reasons –
- It is a structured language that is easy to learn

- It allows performance-effective programming

- It supports low-level programming

- C programs can be compiled on diverse platforms and machines.

Why should we use C?

From the very inception of C, it has been used for system development. Some of the most popular operating systems of today have been created in C. the reason why C is the programming language of choice for such applications is that the code written in C is just as efficient as the same written in assembly language.

To name a few, some of the typical applications of C include –

- Language Compilers

- Operating Systems

- Text Editors

- Assemblers

- Network Drivers

- Print Spoolers

- Databases

- Modern Programs

- Utilities

- Language Interpreters

Prerequisites for Learning C

In order to get started with programming in C, you need a text editor and compiler. The versatility of the C programming language can be adjudged from the fact that a C program file may have 3 to a million lines of code. A typical C file is created using the text editor and saved using the .c extension (Example: sample.c). Owing to the legacy of this programming language, the vi editor or vim is used for writing program files.

You may also use Notepad, Brief or Emacs depending on the platform that you are working on. For example, Notepad is the default text editor you will find on the Windows platform. On the other hand, vi or vim is typically the text editor for Linux and Unix, but it is also available for Windows. Depending on your requirement, you can use the text editor you are most comfortable in working with. The text files that contain your program code are called source files.

Before you move on to the discussion on compiler, make sure you have one text editor installed on your system. If you are good so far, then by now you have a text editor on which you can create a C source file. The next software that you require is a compiler program for compiling and executing the source file. The compiler takes the .c file as input and creates an executable file corresponding to it. This executable file can then be run to execute the program.

The most popular C compiler available is GNU C/C++ compiler. Besides this, you also have compilers from Solaris and HP for their respective configurations. The use of GNU GCC compiler is recommended. If you have Linux or Unix, you can use the compiler in its home environment. However, you may have to install it by following the instructions provided at the GNU GCC compiler.

On the other hand, if you are working on Mac, you will have to download and install Xcode, which allows you to use the GCC for compiling C code and executing the same. Lastly, if you are a Windows user, you cannot directly use GCC unless you install MinGW. However, be sure to install gcc-g++, gcc-core and binutils for a basic setup. To get the programming environment up and running, you will also have to update the PATH variable. Once the installation is complete, you will be able to access GNU tools from the command line of Windows.

Getting Started with C

A standard C program for printing 'Hello World!' is given below.

#include <stdio.h>

int main() {

printf("Hello, World! \n");

    return 0;

}

In order to print the result on the screen, the standard input/output header file stdio.h needs to be included. Execution starts from the main method. This program has the print statement inside the main method. Since, every method in C is expected to return a value, the main method returns 0 on successful completion, which is the last statement of the program. Using a text editor, create a file named sample.c and write this code in it. Compile and execute the file to get the desired result. .

What next?

Now that you are thorough with the basics of C, you can graduate to the book on 'C' for lessons on C programming.

Chapter 6: C++

In continuation with C, a middle-level language called C++ was developed at Bell Labs in the year 1979. Bjarne Stroustrup is credited for the development of this programing language. The biggest advantage of C++ is that it is cross-platform and can be run on Mac, Linux or Windows. Assuming that you have already gone through the chapter on C and programming language concepts, an introduction to C++ should be a cakewalk.

C++ Simplified

C++ includes features from both low-level and high-level languages. Therefore, it has been classified as a middle-level language. Besides this, it supports procedural, generic and object oriented programming. Besides this, C++ is a general purpose, statically typed, free form and case sensitive language. When we say that C++ is statically typed, we mean that type checking is done during compilation and not during runtime.

There are three main components of C++ namely the core language, standard template library and C++ standard library. The core language includes the basics of C++ constructs and programming language elements. The standard template library provides a rich set of methods for manipulation of data structures. For any other kind of structures like files and strings, methods are available in the C++ standard library.

The ANSI standard of C++ emphasizes on code portability. It is a stable version of C++ that ensures error-free compilation of a working C++ code on Windows, Linux, Unix and Linux. It is good to follow the ANSI standard when learning C++. Another important thing that you need to ensure for a smooth learning pathway is to focus on concepts more than constructs.

Applications of C++ Programming

C++ has found applications in almost every application domain. With that said, some of the atypical uses of C++ include device drivers or any software that requires dealing with hardware on a direct, one-to-one basis. Besides this, the user interfaces of most operating systems including that of Macintosh and Windows have been written in C++.

Prerequisites for Learning C++

In order to create, compile and run C++ programs, you need two tools. Firstly, you need a text editor. This shall be used for creating C++ code file, which are typically saved with the extension .cpp. If you are a Windows user, you can stick to Notepad, else you may try EMACS or vi/vim.

Once you have your C++ code files ready, you need to compile them for execution. For this, you need a C++ compiler. The use of GNU C/C++ compiler is highly recommended as it is completely based on the ANSI standard of C++. So, if you are following the ANSI standard, you will not see unnecessary warning or unwarranted errors.

Getting Started with C++

A sample C++ program is given below. This program, upon successful execution, prints 'Hello World!' on the screen.

```
#include <iostream>

using namespace std;

int main()

{

        cout << "Hello World";

        return 0;
```

```
}
```

The structure and constructs of C++ are similar to that of C. There is a main method that includes the code to be executed. The header file, iostream, needs to be included for input/output operations. C++ introduces the concept of namespaces. This program works within the namespace std, which includes all the inbuilt libraries and functionalities.

All you need to do is write this code in a text file and save it with the extension .cpp. Compile this file using GNU C/C++ compiler and execute to see how this code fairs.

What next?

For more lessons on C++ programming, we recommend you to take up our book on 'C++' and get all the information you require to build your expertise in this area of programming.

Chapter 7: C#

Microsoft developed C# as an object-oriented, simple, general purpose, modern programming language as part of its .NET initiative. Anders Hejlsberg headed the development process. It is possible for beginners to start from scratch and become experts on C# with no knowledge of C or any other programming language for that matter.

However, a basic understanding of programming language concepts is certainly recommended before starting your C# journey. Besides this, if you have experience in C or C++, learning C# will be quicker and smoother. You can set up s system for C# programming exercises and practice. In case, it is not possible for you to make any such arrangements, you can also try the online compilers and execution environments to sail through the learning process.

What's new in C#?

It was during the development of .NET framework that C# was created and it went on to bag approvals form International Standards Organization (ISO) and European Computer Manufacturers Association (ECMA). The motive behind the design of this language was to develop a Common Language Infrastructure (CLI). This infrastructure was expected to include a runtime environment and executable code. As a result, codes written in high-level languages could be run on diverse platforms and systems.

Key features of C# are as follows –
- A component of .NET Framework.
- Modern
- Object oriented.

- General-purpose

- Easy to learn.

- Component oriented.

- Leads to improved efficiency in programs

- Structured language.

- Cross-platform

Although, C# is the last in the league of C and C++ programming languages, it also shares ground with Java. The strong programming features that C# provides developers makes it a popular and widely–used programming language. Some specific programming features available in C# include –

- Automatic Garbage Collection

- Boolean Conditions

- Assembly Versioning

- Standard Library

- Properties and Events

- Delegates and Events Management

- Indexers

- Easy-to-use Generics

- Simple Multithreading

- Conditional Compilation

- Integration with Windows

- LINQ and Lambda Expressions

Prerequisites for Learning C#

Like we mentioned previously, C# was developed as part of the .NET project. Therefore, in order to understand C# and its components, it is important to know what .NET framework is and what it does. Fundamentally, .NET framework is a platform that facilitates development of web services, web applications and windows applications.

The multi-language support of this platform allows programmers to use it from many languages like C++, COBOL, Visual Basic and Jscript, in addition to C#. Besides this, the framework also allows all these languages to communicate with each other. In a nutshell, you must have the latest version of .NET framework on your system before you can think of installing Integrated Development Environments (IDEs) for C# programming.

The tools provided by Microsoft for C# programming include Visual Web Developer, Visual C# 2010 Express and Visual Studio 2010. The first two tools namely Visual Web Developer and Visual C# 2010 Studio are free and can be used for C# programming. If you don't wish to use an IDE, you can also use the text editor to create C# code files. These files can be compiled and executed from the command line using the compiler that is available as part of the .NET framework.

It is noteworthy to mention here that .NET was developed for Windows by Microsoft and .NET installation, with or without IDE integration will allow you to perform C# programming on Windows. However, if you are Linux or Mac user, you will need Mono, which is a .NET framework's open-source version. It includes a compiler for C# and can be used on almost all other platforms.

Getting Started with C# Programming

You cannot say that you have completed a lesson on programming unless you see and understand a code snippet. To help you get the look and feel of C# programming, we have included a basic program. This program prints the phrase 'Hello World!' on the screen upon execution.

```
using System;

namespace MyHelloWorld

{

        class SampleHelloWorld

        {

                static void main(string[] args)

                {

                        Console.WriteLine("Hello World!");

                        Console.ReadKey();

                }

        }

}
```

In line with the object oriented principles, C#, like C++ also implements and uses the concept of namespaces. A namespace is nothing, but a boundary. When you are working in a namespace, you have access to elements allowed in that namespace. The second thing that you will notice in the code written above is the class construct is created for the application.

Inside the class construct, the main method is defined, which contains code for printing the string. The last statement waits for the user to hit any key before the execution window terminates. If you omit this statement, your program will run fine, but you will not be able to see the window with the result. You can write this code in a text file and name it main.cs. Compile and execute the file to get the desired result.

What next?

The sample program provided above is just a glimpse of how C# code looks. Learning C# and gaining expertise in it is a long journey that begins from this small code snippet. To get a comprehensive course on C# programming, we recommend you to pick up our book on 'C#'.

Chapter 8: Python

Python is a general-purpose language that is interpreted and not compiled. Moreover, it is a high-level language that works on the object-oriented model and the developer has immense control over program as interactions between the developer and interpreter are supported via the command prompt. Python was developed during the period 1985-1990 and Guido van Rossum is credited for its existence.

Just like Perl, the source code of Python is also available under the GNU General Public License (GPL). This chapter shall introduce you to this programming language. For advanced lessons on Python programming, you are recommended to follow the book 'Python'.

Before you begin, it is crucial for you to realize that beginners just as well as programmers can easily learn this programming language. So, if you have a basic understanding of programming concepts, you are expected to have a smooth learning curve. However, if you don't have any past experience in programming, this is the place you can start your programming journey from.

Python Essentials

The biggest USP of Python is the fact that it is highly readable. It appears like simple English language instructions given to a layman. As opposed to other programming languages, Python uses English words much more often than punctuations. As a result, the syntactical constructions in Python are way lesser as compared to other programming languages.

Python is best described using the keywords, 'object-oriented', interactive', 'high-level' and 'interpreted' general-purpose language. The key features of Python dig deeper into these keywords and they are relevant for your understanding of Python.

Interpreted, not compiled!
The python code is not compiled and is directly interpreted by the interpreter at runtime and executed. This property makes Python codes more efficient and lightweight.

Supports interaction with the interpreter
Python gives the power to code and execute completely and absolutely to the programmer. You can literally interact with the interpreter for writing python programs via the Python prompt.

Object Oriented
This programming language is based on the object-oriented methodology. It supports the fundamental OOPs concept of encapsulation and all the code is encapsulated and presented in the form of objects.

Truly, a Beginner's Language!
No programming language is as simple as Python yet it allows the programmers to develop programs ranging from simple text processing to browsers. So, if you are a beginner, you can get started with the simple programs and graduate to advance programming concepts to become an expert.

How did it all begin?

National Research Institute for Mathematics and Computer Science, Netherlands' Guido van Rossum is credited for the development of Python. Python was developed around late eighties and is known to have been derived from many programming languages like C++, Modula-3, C, ABC, Smalltalk, Unix and Algol-68, besides many others.

Although, Python is a copyrighted language, you can access the source code as it has been made available under GNU General Public License (GPL). This programming language continues to grow and evolve and Guido van Rossum still directs and monitors its progress. However, the responsibility of maintenance of the core lies with a core development team now.

Features

Python is a feature-packed programming language. Some of the key features of this programming language include –

Readable

Python is one of the rare programming language is just as simple to write as it is to write.

Easy and Simple

The syntax for Python is clearly defined and the structures and keywords are crisp and lesser in number. So, you have all that you need without the extras or add-ons that other programming languages have.

Maintainable

Considering the high readability of this programming language, it doesn't suffer from the issues that plague the other complicated languages. It is possible to change, alter and maintain the Python code by more than one programmer without much of an issue.

Interactive

One of the biggest USPs of Python is that it allows the developer to interact with the execution process via the interactive shell. Therefore, the developer can test code and debug snippets of code interactively.

Portable

Python is independent of the hardware and software platform of the base system in the sense that it provides an interface for almost all software platforms. This makes this programming language extremely portable.

Rich Library

The portability of this language clubbed with a power-packed library allows the developers to make use of the benefits of an in-built library on any system, be it Windows, Unix or Mac.

Extendable

The tools can be enhanced and customized by the programmer according to his or her needs by adding low-level modules to the interpreter of Python. This allows programmers to develop efficient and optimized code specific to every application.

Database Support

Database support is one of the most crucial features for any programming language considering the shift of application niche to data-intensive applications. In line with this requirement, Python provides support in the form of interfaces to most of the popular and commercial databases used today.

Scalable

Considering the simplicity of this programming language, it can easily manage large programs without disturbing the structure of the program.

GUI Programming

Python allows creation and porting of GUI applications to Windows systems, libraries and system calls.

In addition to the key features mentioned above, Python has a host of other features to its credit. These features are as follows –

- Garbage is automatically collected by the Python system.

- You can create programs based on structured as well as OOPs approach of programming.

- Python fits in as the language of choice for large applications just as well as for scripting.

- Python supports dynamic data types, which are type-checked dynamically.

- The code created in Python can be integrated with Java, C++, CORBA, ActiveX, COM as well as C.

Prerequisites for Learning Python

Python programming can be performed on a range of platforms like Mac, Windows, Linux and Unix. However, before you can actually sit down and do programming in Python, you will need to prepare your system. Most systems have Python pre-installed. SO, it is best to open the command prompt and type 'python' to check if the software is already there and if it is there, the version of the same that is in use.

The platforms supported by Python include –

- Win 9x/NT/2000
- Linux
- Unix
- OS/2
- Macintosh (Intel, PPC, 68K)
- PalmOS
- DOS (multiple versions)
- Windows CE
- Nokia mobile phones
- BeOS
- Acorn/RISC OS
- VMS/OpenVMS
- Amiga
- VxWorks
- QNX
- Java and .NET VMs
- Psion

In order to install Python and get a copy of its documentation, you can visit the official website of Python. All you need to do is follow the instructions provided for installation to your software platform and you should be good to go. In all probability, you will get the byte-code that you will need to directly install. However, if you don't get the byte code, you will need to compile the code using a C compiler to get the byte code. If you need to customize the installation and choose the features you wish to install, you have the flexibility to do so using the compiling option. Be sure to set the path variables for your system to get the system running for you.

If you like to work with integrated development environments (IDEs), Python provides you this option as well. You can run Python through a graphical user interface using one of the following IDEs –

- Unix IDE for Python on a Unix system

- PythonWin for Windows

- IDLE IDE for Mac

If you face issues during and after the installation, it is best to consult an expert. However, do not jump to Python programming unless you have the system up and running. Apart from the desktop options, you may also try the online option. There are many portals that allow you to code and test in Python for free. You can explore this option for a makeshift arrangement until your system gets ready.

Getting Started with Python

Here is a sample code for you to try.

#!/usr/bin/python

print "Hello World!"

Write this code in a text file and save it as main.py. Execute the code by writing main.py on the python command prompt to get the desired result.

What next?

Moving on, you can follow the book on 'Python' for a detailed understanding of this beautiful programming language. This book contains basic and advance programming lessons and is highly recommended for first-time learners as well as experts.

Chapter 9: HTML

The name HTML is synonymous with webpages and the web today. If you have had the opportunity to create a webpage or see the source code of the same, you must have realized that most webpages are created in HTML. So, what is HTML, what does it stand for, how did it come into existence and what all you need to know to code in HTML? We will answer all these queries for you in this chapter.

Berners-Lee created Hyper Text Markup Language (HTML) in 1991. However, it was four years later in the 1995 that the language was standardized and released in the form of HTML 2.0. One of the first major versions of this language was released in 1999 under the name HTML 4.01. Most of the present day HTML programming is done in HTML 5.0, which is an extended version of HTML 4.01. This version came into being in the year 2012.

This language is the language for you is you are an aspiring web developer or designer. You can't work with webpages unless you have a clear understanding of what makes them and how they work. We shall give you all the ingredients you need to learn the language and develop a higher level of expertise in the same.

HTML Fundamentals

As we mentioned previously, the commonly used programming language for webpage development is HTML. Let us now expand the acronym and go into the details of each of the words 'Hyper Text Markup Language'.

- The link that you see on one webpage to go to another page is 'hypertext' and this forms the basis of how webpages are linked together.

- HTML is a markup language. Therefore, all that HTML does is create markups in the form of tags that are read by the browser and the browser directly comes to know how the webpage is to be displayed.

The intent behind the development of HTML was to create a language that can clearly define document structure by declaring headings, paragraphs, lists and other components of the documents. This was made for the scientific community to allow them to share scientific information easily. However, as time passed, HTML found application in webpage structuring.

Prerequisites for Learning HTML

Before beginning the HTML tutorial, you need to have a clear understanding of the Windows or Linux operating system. On the system of your choice, you must have worked with a text editor (Notepad for Windows or TextEdit for Linux). Besides this, you must be able to create directories and subdirectories.

File organization is the base of HTML programming and will determine the navigation path of your website. Be sure to be thorough with these concepts before you begin. Lastly, you must be acquainted with the different file formats used for images like JPEG, GIF, PNG and TIF.

If you face issues in running HTML code and examples on the local system, you can search for HTML editors online and use the one that best suits your understanding and level.

Creating Your First HTML Document

A simple HTML document will typically look like this –

<!DOCTYPE html>

<html>

<head>

 <title>Sample HTML Page</title>

</head>

<body>

<h1>Sample Heading</h1>

<p>My first paragraph..</p>

</body>

</html>

You can directly write this code in the online HTML editor. Alternatively, if you wish to run this HTML code on your system, you need to open the Notepad and write this HTML code in it. Once you are done, save the file with the name sample1.htm. You can keep any filename you like, but be sure to use the extension .htm. Lastly, open the file using any browser installed on your system and you will be able to see the webpage you created with the heading and paragraph you mentioned. Try out a few variations to see how editing HTML changes the webpage.

Tags in HTML

Now that you have already created your first HTML page, it is time for you to understand what the HTML code written above means. Like we mentioned previously, HTML is a markup language. Therefore, it marks up webpages with the help of tags to tell the browser how the webpage should look. Typically, a tag is enclosed inside angle braces. Therefore, anything of the format, <tag-name>, is a tag.

With a few exceptions, every tag will have an opening tag and a corresponding closing tag. For instance, you can see in your webpage that <html> and </html> both exist. While former is the opening tag, latter is the closing tag. Similarly, tags like <head>, <title>, <body> and <p> are opening tags with </head>, </title>, </body> and </p> being their corresponding closing tags. Starting from HTML 4, the World Wide Web Consortium (W3C) has recommended the use of lowercase letters for writing tags. So, the use of lowercase letters is intentional.

The tags used in the webpage shown above are as follows –

<!DOCTYPE...>
This is the first tag in every HTML page and is indicative of the type of document and the version of HTML being used.

html
The rest of the html document is enclosed with the <html> tag indicating that the document is an HTML document and all the contents that lie within this tag need to be read and displayed by the browser in the form of HTML.

head
The HTML document created above is divided into two main parts namely header, body and footer. The first part of the page contains the heading of the page title. This is indicated by the tag <head></head>. All the contents within this tag are treated as header by the browser.

title
This is a tag that is written inside the <head></head> tag to indicate the title of the document.

body
The second part of the webpage is the document body and is typically enclosed inside the tags <body> and </body>. Divisions of text and paragraphs fall under this document section.

h1
HTML supports multi-level headings. The first level of heading (the biggest in font size among all the headings) is enclosed within the tags, <h1> and </h1>. These tags appear inside the body tag of the HTML document.

_p_

Paragraphs in the HTML document are a part of the body and are enclosed inside the <body></body>. Any text that needs to be displayed as a paragraph can be enclosed with the tags <p> and </p>.

What next?

We have only discussed basic tags. It is evident from the amazing webpages that are active on the Internet today that HTML supports a lot of functionalities and there are corresponding tags to build that functionality. While this has given you an insight on what you are getting into, you will need to learn the other tags and structures of HTML before you can formally call yourself a web developer. You can refer to our book on 'HTML' for basic and advanced lessons on this programming language.

Chapter 10: CSS

While HTML structures documents and tells the browser the components of the webpage and the order and way in which they have to be displayed, the pages created using only HTML are rather raw. The webpage that we created in the last chapter displayed the content in the order and manner we wanted, but it was far from the beautifully styled pages that can be seen in the Internet world today. So, what gives webpages the functionality and style? While JavaScript is the programming language that allows webpages to do all that they are capable of doing, CSS takes care of the styling part.

The full form of CSS is Cascading Style Sheet. The first version of CSS was called CSS1, after which CSS 2 was released and presently, we are working on CSS3. This programming language is a must to know for anyone who wants to play around with webpages, from developers to designers and learners to experts. An expertise on CSS shall take your webpage development to a much higher level.

CSS Basics

It would not be wrong to say that CSS is a programming language for designing. Therefore, it is just as much a design language as it is a programming language. CSS was created with the intent to simplify the process of beautifying webpages. Therefore, Cascading Style Sheets or CSS is a simple language for designing webpages.

While HTML gives a webpage its structure, CSS gives it the look and feel that it should have for people to visit the webpage and keep coming back to it. CSS allows you to control the font-style, font-size, color, layout, screen sizes and spacing between lines and paragraphs. Besides this, the use of images and effects in the background, foreground or anywhere on the webpage for that matter can be controlled and styled using CSS.

With the amount of power that CSS instills into the web developer to create the webpage he or she has imagined, its simplicity is surely worth a mention. It is a powerful yet simple language. With that said, CSS can be used only on webpages already created using HTML or XHTML.

Hakon Wium Lie created CSS in 1994. Since then, it has been maintained by W3C, which is also popularly known as the CSS Working Group. This group is responsible for updating CSS and release specifications, which are recommendations or ratified specifications from the W3C members. It is a formal document released on a regular basis.

The recommendations are made to developers and companies. However, the group or W3C has no control over how the recommendations will be implemented. It is the same working group that makes recommendations on how the Internet should work and evolve over time.

The world has seen three versions of CSS till date. The first version or CSS1 was released as a recommendation by W3C in the year 1996. This version of CSS was described as a simple visual formatting language to be used for all HTML tags. The second version (CSS2) came two years later in 1998 and added support for media-specific styling. The latest version (CSS3) was released in 1999, which is a feature-rich version of its predecessors. It was released in the form of modules, which are as follows –

- User Interface
- Box Model
- Selectors
- Image Values and Replaced Content
- Backgrounds and Borders

- 2D/3D Transformations

- Text Effects

- Multiple Column Layout

- Animations

Key Advantages of Using CSS

CSS offers several reasons and advantages to the web developer. Some of these include –

Time saving
The fact that you need to create CSS sheets once and then you can use them anywhere according to your requirement, implements code reuse in the most exemplary manner. You can create a style and use it for styling many webpages. This saves a lot of time.

Efficient webpages
The use of CSS has a positive impact on reducing download times, as you no longer have to write tags along with its attributes every single time. You can declare a CSS rule and apply this rule to the tag. This reduces the amount of code written on the HTML document. Thus, the download time is also reduced.

Easy to maintain
Since you are creating style sheets and just applying the style sheet to the webpage, you can make global changes easily by editing the style sheet. Moreover, a bad change can be undone easily as you don't have to go through the HTML code for it.

Professional styling
HTML gives a raw look to the webpage. The beauty and user-friendliness of the webpage are enhanced only with the use of CSS. Considering the fundamental requirement of user-friendliness in web applications and portals, the use of CSS is inevitable.

Multi-device compatibility

Nowadays, webpages and web applications are not just created for desktop viewing, they need to be optimized for mobiles and PDAs as well. Styling sheets facilitate styling and optimization of the HTML document for different viewing experiences.

Supports offline browsing

The ability of CSS to store web applications on the local cache allows developers to support offline viewing. This gives immense competitive advantage to webpages as holding onto an ongoing experience is much simpler that expecting a return viewing experience.

Works for all browsers

CSS is platform-independent in the sense that all latest browsers support CSS well.

Changing global standards

As HTML is evolving, tags and attributes are being deprecated and developers are advised to use CSS for styling. In line with this trend, all future browsers are expected to work on this principle and any webpage that you create with CSS todays is more likely to be compatible with future browsers.

Prerequisites for Learning CSS

Evidently, CSS is a programming language that works over and above HTML. Therefore, a basic understanding of HTML and XHTML can be of great help. Besides this, you should have some experience in working with web browsers, text editors, files and directories.

You can use the operating system of your choice. No matter which platform you choose to work on, be sure to have a text editor and browser of your choice installed on it. Besides this, just like HTML, file organization, working with directories and subdirectories and navigation between directories is crucial for CSS learning.

What next?

Now that you have a basic understanding of CSS and what it can do with your raw HTML webpages, you can take this learning further with our book on 'CSS' and create beautiful webpages that are sure to get you compliments and accolades.

Chapter 11: JavaScript

In line with our discussion on languages that are interpreted and not compiled, the next language that we will discuss is JavaScript. The primary objective behind developing this language is creation of network-centric applications. This programming language is an add-on for Java and can be easily integrated with it. Moreover, it compliments the abilities of core Java in the best possible manner.

JavaScript Explained

The most important feature of JavaScript is its light-weightiness and dynamicity. This allows it easy integration with webpages without affecting the performance of the system. The dynamicity of this programming language allows integration of the JavaScript program into the client-side webpage, allowing clean interactions between the user and system. All of this comes with innate object oriented capabilities and interpreter-enabled execution.

The first name given to this programming language was LiveScript, which was released as such in the year 1995. However, after the popularity of Java, Netscape decided to change the name to a catchier JavaScript. Several web browsers like Internet Explorer and Netscape have an inbuilt-core for this language.

The core JavaScript language was standardized by ECMA-262 specification, listing the following key features –

- It is open source
- Easy implement due to similarities and integration with HTML
- Easy integration with Java and complements the language
- Easy integration with HTML and complements the language

- It is cross-platform

- It is light-weight

- It is interpreted, not compiled

- It is designed for development of applications centered on the network.

Both, Microsoft's Jscript and Netscape's JavaScript abide by the standards set by ECMAScript standard. However, both these versions of JavaScript also support features that are not listed in the standard guidelines.

Client-side Scripting Using JavaScript

JavaScript is tailor-made for client-side scripting. It needs to be integrated in the HTML of the webpage or the webpage must refer to the same for inclusion. The browser automatically interprets the script after integration of JavaScript with HTML.

The inclusion of JavaScript to the HTML page transforms it from a static page to a dynamic page that can communicate with the user and control the operations of the browser. Besides this, JavaScript also allows creation of HTML content for the page in a dynamic manner. The use of JavaScript has several advantages over its counterparts.

A common example where JavaScript is used at the client-side is form filling. A JavaScript can be included into the webpage to check if the user has entered all the fields with valid entries before the form can be submitted to the server for further execution.

For instance, fields like date will have to be in a valid format for processing. This can be checked at the client end, before the submission of the form to the server, to avoid unnecessary overheads. As a result, the webpage becomes light and dynamic, both at the same time.

Besides this, user's interaction with the page in the form of navigation and button clicks can also be managed with ease using

JavaScript. This includes explicit and implicit actions initiated by the user.

Key Advantages of Using JavaScript

Low webpage response time
Since the Script runs locally on the client side, the interaction can be checked and pre-processed locally. It is only when the server's intervention is absolutely necessary that the server is contacted. As a result, the response time of the webpage is substantially improved.

Reduced interaction required between the webpage and server
The JavaScript embedded in the client webpage can check minor tasks like error checking of the user input. This reduces the number of requests sent to the server, saving on server traffic. Moreover, the load of the server is also considerably reduced.

Allows development of highly interactive webpages
JavaScript allows tracking of the minutest of activities of the user. Therefore, you can accordingly program the script to react to user input for healthy interaction between the user and system.

The interfaces are richer than ever before
JavaScript allows inclusion of sliders and 'drag and drop' components to the webpage, which gives a richer and more attractive look to the webpage.

Are there any limitations?

As is the case with all technologies, there is a point beyond which the technology fails to work. JavaScript is no exception to this rule. This is perhaps the reason why JavaScript is not even treated like a full-fledged programming language. Some of the features that this programming language lacks include –

- JavaScript's client side scripting ability does not allow you to read and write text file. Although, this feature has been included to prevent security issues that may arise due to its inclusion, this may seem like a limitation to some people.

- JavaScript lacks networking capabilities.

- JavaScript lacks the support for multithreading and multiprocessing.

Development Tools

The availability of low-cost development tools is one of the key reasons why JavaScript has attained the popularity that it has. All you need to get started is a simple text editor program like Notepad. In view of the fact that JavaScript is an interpreted language, you don't even need a compiler to get started with your programs.

With that said, several JavaScript editing tools are also available for your help. One of the most popular tools of this league is Microsoft FrontPage that allows you to edit HTML pages. It also comes bundled with JavaScript tools that can be used to make the webpages better and highly functional.

In addition to this, Macromedia Dreamweaver MX and Macromedia HomeSite 5 are also available. Owing to the availability of many prebuilt JavaScript components, support for XML/XHTML and easy integration with existing databases, Dreamweaver is usually the tool of choice for professional web developers. On the other hand, HomeSite is a good editor for management of personal websites.

Prerequisites for Learning JavaScript

JavaScript is the programming language of choice for programmers who wish to create dynamic webpages or applications with ease and finesse. The prerequisites for learning

JavaScript are some prior knowledge of HTML and how webpages are created in the same.

Besides this, basic knowledge about online applications development and object oriented programming concepts can also be of great help. One of the best ways to practice JavaScript programming is to use one of the online platforms for execution. This shall give you a real-world experience of how your webpages and online applications will look after development.

Getting Started with JavaScript

Since JavaScript is embedded inside HTML documents, you need to create a HTML document first. A sample JavaScript is given here for our understanding and trial.

```
<html>
  <body>
    <script language="javascript" type="text/javascript">
      <!--
        document.write("Hello World!")
      //-->
    </script>
  </body>
</html>
```

Since you are already aware about HTML document creation, the only tag that will be new to you here is that of <script>...</script>. This tag is used to embed scripts inside the HTML document. You can write this code in a text file and save it as samplepage.htm. Open this page using any browser to see what you get as output.

What next?

With the basic introduction to the language, you can go ahead and pick up our book on 'JavaScript' for learning the key concepts and programming in this language.

Conclusion

This book is an introduction to programming language concepts and key programming languages being used todays. While the first few chapters focus on programming concepts and on building a foundation for writing, executing and using programs for personal use, the rest of the book presents a dedicated chapter on the programming languages – Java, JavaScript, C, Python, SQL, HTML and CSS.

Each of these chapters gives a brief introduction to the programming language and should help you head start your course on the programming language. Taking this knowledge forward, you can take up books written for basic and advanced programming for each of these languages to build an expertise in the programming language of your choice.

We hope you enjoyed this book and that it has helped you lay a strong foundation for your future endeavors. Programming is an art and art requires passion! Create the zeal and zest to think out of the box and create something that will be of use to the world. Happy programming!

27766053R00043

Made in the USA
Columbia, SC
28 September 2018